The Complete Inside Story of HBO's Most Anticipated Show

Exploring the Vision, Controversies, and Promises of the Seven-Season Series

LINDSEY T. GORDON

The Complete Inside Story of HBO's Most Anticipated Show

COPYRIGHT

All rights reserved. No part of this publication may be reproduced, distributed, or transmitted in any form or by any means, including photocopying, recording, or other electronic or mechanical methods, without the prior written permission of the publisher, except in the case of brief quotations embodied in critical reviews and certain other noncommercial uses permitted by copyright law.

Copyright © Lindsey T. Gordon, 2024.

The Complete Inside Story of HBO's Most Anticipated Show

TABLE OF CONTENTS

INTRODUCTION..................................... 7
The Magic Returns: HBO's Vision for a New "Harry Potter" Era........................ 7
   Why the Story of a Seven-Season Series Matters Now............................ 9

CHAPTER ONE................................. **14**
Genesis of the Seven-Season Adaptation... 14
   HBO's Rationale: Reviving a Classic for a New Generation............ 16
   A Decade in the Making: Early Discussions and Development.......... 19

CHAPTER TWO................................ **24**
J.K. Rowling's Involvement and Influence.. 24
   Balancing Act: Her Creative Insights vs. Public Backlash.............. 27
   A Longstanding Partnership: Rowling and HBO's Two-Decade Collaboration..................................... 30

The Complete Inside Story of HBO's Most Anticipated Show

CHAPTER THREE................................34
Casting Harry, Ron, and Hermione for a New Era.. 34
   Challenges and Expectations: Filling Iconic Roles........................... 37
   Fan Reactions: Enthusiasm and Skepticism About Diverse Casting.. 40

CHAPTER FOUR.................................44
Controversies and Conversations Around Inclusivity................................. 44
   HBO's Commitment to Diversity: Navigating Public Criticism............... 47
   The Broader Cultural Landscape: Gender Identity in Media Today...50

CHAPTER FIVE...................................54
Crafting a Faithful Adaptation............... 54
   Revisiting Key Themes: Friendship, Courage, and Acceptance...57
   Adapting for the Screen: Challenges of Long-Form Storytelling.. 61

The Complete Inside Story of HBO's Most Anticipated Show

CHAPTER SIX 65
The Creative Team Behind the Magic 65
   Collaborating with Original Film Talent: A Legacy Connection 68
   New Faces, Fresh Perspectives: The Producers' Vision 71

CHAPTER SEVEN 76
Production Design and World-Building 76
   Special Effects in a New Era: Advancements in Technology 80
   Costume and Set Design: Evoking Magic Through Detail 84

CHAPTER EIGHT 89
Fan Reactions and Divided Opinions 89
   Online Backlash: The Role of Social Media in Shaping Perceptions 94
   Balancing Legacy and Progress: The Show's Responsibility 99

CHAPTER NINE............ 104
Industry Implications and HBO's High Stakes............ 104
Financial and Cultural Investments: What's on the Line for HBO............ 108
Lessons from the Past: How Other Reboots Have Fared............ 112

CHAPTER TEN............118
A Look Ahead to 2027 and Beyond............ 118
The Evolution of the Harry Potter Legacy: A New Chapter Begins............ 121
Speculation and Hopes: What Fans Want from Seven Seasons............ 125

CONCLUSION............ 131
The Power of Stories: Why the New Harry Potter Series Matters............ 131
Bridging the Gap: Fandom, Inclusion, and the Magic of Adaptation............ 134

INTRODUCTION

The Magic Returns: HBO's Vision for a New "Harry Potter" Era

When HBO announced its plan to adapt J.K. Rowling's iconic "Harry Potter" series into a seven-season television event, it reignited the fervor of a global fanbase that had grown up immersed in the magic of Hogwarts. This ambitious project signals a significant moment for both the franchise and the entertainment industry at large. HBO, renowned for its prestige programming and unparalleled production values, is betting big on bringing the wizarding world to life once more.

At its core, the series promises to be a "faithful adaptation" of Rowling's original works, diving deeper into the complex narratives, character arcs, and intricate details that were only touched upon in the films. The episodic format allows for unparalleled storytelling potential, ensuring that fans can savor the richness of the source material without the time constraints of a two-hour movie.

HBO's vision goes beyond simply recreating the magic—it aims to modernize it while remaining deeply rooted in the themes that made the books timeless. Friendship, courage, love, and the triumph of good over evil resonate universally, and the series seeks to reintroduce these ideas to a new generation of viewers. By committing to an inclusive casting process and state-of-the-art production design, HBO is crafting a show that honors the past while forging a new path forward.

The announcement also signals a strategic play for HBO Max in the streaming wars. As franchises dominate the battle for subscriber loyalty, revisiting "Harry Potter" is not just about storytelling; it's a business move aimed at capturing both nostalgic fans and newcomers. For millions, this series represents a return to a cherished world of enchantment—a chance to reconnect with a story that shaped their childhoods and continues to inspire them.

Why the Story of a Seven-Season Series Matters Now

The decision to adapt "Harry Potter" into a seven-season series couldn't come at a more critical cultural moment. As the entertainment industry grapples with changing audience dynamics, diverse representation, and the impact of polarizing creators, this adaptation is poised to redefine what it means to retell a beloved story.

Firstly, the seven-season structure mirrors the seven books, offering a unique opportunity for expansive world-building and character development. Each season will focus on a single book, allowing the intricate subplots and emotional nuances to unfold organically. For fans who felt that the films glossed over key moments—such as Hermione's activism with S.P.E.W., the depth of Harry's trauma, or the intricacies of Voldemort's Horcruxes—this format promises a richer and more immersive experience.

Secondly, the timing of this adaptation aligns with a generational shift. The original "Harry Potter" films debuted between 2001 and 2011, captivating a generation that is now raising families of their own. For them, this series is an opportunity to share the magic with their children while reliving the wonder through a fresh lens. At the same time, younger viewers who missed the cultural phenomenon of the books and films can experience the story for the first time, tailored to contemporary sensibilities.

Moreover, this adaptation arrives at a juncture where fandom itself is evolving. While Rowling's public statements have sparked heated debates about inclusion and representation, the series aims to transcend controversy by focusing on the universality of the story. HBO's commitment to inclusive casting and its acknowledgment of diverse audiences signal an effort to embrace progress without discarding tradition. This balance between honoring the source material and modernizing its presentation underscores the relevance of the story today.

Finally, the project highlights the enduring appeal of "Harry Potter" as a cultural and literary phenomenon. In a world grappling with division, uncertainty, and rapid change, the themes of the series—hope, resilience, and the power of unity—feel more resonant than ever. By revisiting Hogwarts, HBO invites us to believe in the possibility of magic once more, reminding us that even in the darkest times, there is light to be found.

The seven-season series isn't just about nostalgia; it's a reflection of how stories evolve and adapt to meet the needs of their time. Through this ambitious undertaking, HBO aims to prove that the magic of "Harry Potter" is far from over—it's just beginning a new chapter.

CHAPTER ONE

Genesis of the Seven-Season Adaptation

The official announcement of a "Harry Potter" television series in April 2023 was a watershed moment for the franchise and its fans. HBO, under its streaming platform Max, unveiled plans for an unprecedented seven-season series that would revisit J.K. Rowling's beloved wizarding world in a format tailored for today's streaming-dominated media landscape.

The news was met with a mixture of excitement and skepticism. For long-time fans, the promise of a "faithful adaptation" of the books rekindled a sense of nostalgia, offering hope that details omitted from the original films—such as the Marauders' backstory or the full complexity of Snape's character—would finally get their due. However, it also raised questions about whether the magic of the original films could be recaptured and how the show would navigate the controversies surrounding Rowling's personal views.

HBO's announcement coincided with a strategic move to establish Max as a heavyweight in the increasingly competitive streaming market. The timing was deliberate, positioning the series as a cornerstone of Max's content library. In the official press release, executives described the series as a "decade-long commitment," signaling the network's confidence in "Harry

Potter"'s enduring appeal and its potential to draw a multigenerational audience.

The announcement also promised to revisit the books with a fresh perspective, utilizing advancements in storytelling, technology, and representation to reimagine the series for modern viewers. As social media buzzed with debates, predictions, and fan theories, it became clear that this adaptation was poised to reignite the global fascination with Rowling's magical universe.

HBO's Rationale: Reviving a Classic for a New Generation

The decision to embark on a seven-season adaptation was driven by a confluence of artistic, cultural, and commercial factors. For HBO, "Harry Potter" represented more than just a nostalgic franchise; it was a narrative powerhouse with the capacity to connect with audiences of all ages.

The original films, while beloved, were constrained by the medium's time limits. Key elements of Rowling's novels—such as the intricacies of Voldemort's Horcruxes, Harry's evolving psychological struggles, and the moral gray areas of characters like Dumbledore—were necessarily streamlined or omitted entirely. With a seven-season format, HBO saw an opportunity to restore the depth and complexity of the books, offering fans a richer and more authentic experience.

Furthermore, the adaptation allowed HBO to bridge the generational gap. Millennials who grew up with the books and films are now adults, and many are eager to share the magic with their children. At the same time, younger viewers, accustomed to serialized storytelling through platforms like Netflix and Disney+, are a prime audience for a long-form narrative that delves deeply into the world of Hogwarts.

Culturally, the series provides a platform to revisit themes that remain profoundly relevant today. The values of courage, friendship, and the fight against systemic oppression resonate in a world grappling with issues of division and inequality. By revisiting these themes, HBO aimed to position "Harry Potter" not just as an escapist fantasy, but as a story with real-world implications and lessons for its audience.

Finally, from a commercial standpoint, the timing was ideal. The rise of franchise-driven content, as seen with Disney's Marvel and Star Wars expansions, underscored the importance of leveraging intellectual property with global recognition. For HBO, "Harry Potter" was a natural choice—an established brand with a built-in fanbase that could be further revitalized through strategic updates and marketing.

A Decade in the Making: Early Discussions and Development

While the announcement in 2023 made headlines, the groundwork for the "Harry Potter" television series had been quietly laid years earlier. Internal discussions at Warner Bros. and HBO reportedly began as early as the mid-2010s, spurred by the enduring popularity of the franchise and the success of spinoffs like "Fantastic Beasts" and "The Cursed Child."

However, initial proposals faced significant hurdles. J.K. Rowling, who retained creative control over her intellectual property, was cautious about overextending the franchise. She was particularly insistent that any adaptation remain faithful to the original books and their core themes. This led to protracted negotiations, as both sides worked to ensure the integrity of the story while adapting it for a modern audience.

Technological advancements also played a role in delaying the project. Executives wanted to wait until production capabilities could match the grandeur of Rowling's vision. Innovations in CGI, virtual production, and set design over the past decade made it possible to envision a Hogwarts that felt more immersive and dynamic than ever before.

In parallel, HBO undertook extensive market research to gauge audience interest and expectations. The findings were clear: fans wanted a deeper exploration of the books' narratives, more diverse representation, and a commitment to high-quality storytelling. This feedback shaped the project's scope and direction, ensuring that it would meet the high standards set by both fans and the network.

By the time the series was announced, HBO had assembled a preliminary creative team, including writers and producers with a deep understanding of the franchise. J.K. Rowling's direct involvement as an executive producer added an additional layer of authenticity, ensuring that the adaptation would stay true to her original vision.

Ultimately, the genesis of the seven-season adaptation was the result of years of careful planning, collaboration, and a shared commitment to reimagining "Harry Potter" for a new era. It was a project born from both a reverence for the past and a belief in the story's power to inspire future generations.

CHAPTER TWO

J.K. Rowling's Involvement and Influence

J.K. Rowling's role as an executive producer on HBO's "Harry Potter" series is both pivotal and emblematic of her enduring influence on the franchise. As the original author and creator of the wizarding world, Rowling's involvement ensures that the series remains authentic to the core vision of her books. Her intimate knowledge of the story's complexities, characters, and underlying themes positions her as an irreplaceable creative force within the project.

In her capacity as executive producer, Rowling has been deeply involved in major creative decisions. From selecting the showrunner and writers to reviewing early scripts, her input has been instrumental in shaping the direction of the series. Reports indicate that she has played a hands-on role in ensuring that the adaptation captures the full scope of her novels, advocating for elements that were either condensed or omitted in the films. For instance, Rowling has expressed interest in exploring Harry's psychological trauma, the intricacies of magical lore, and the socio-political undercurrents of the wizarding world.

Beyond the narrative, Rowling's involvement extends to the casting process and overall creative vision. She has reportedly collaborated with the team to identify actors who can bring depth and nuance to the iconic roles of Harry, Ron, Hermione, and others. Her insistence on aligning the show's tone with the books' progressive maturation—starting with the innocence of "The Sorcerer's Stone" and gradually moving into the darker territory of "The Deathly Hallows"—is a testament to her commitment to doing justice to the source material.

For HBO, Rowling's presence as an executive producer adds a layer of legitimacy to the project. Fans have long debated whether the magic of the original story could be replicated without her involvement, and her direct participation helps assuage concerns about the series' authenticity. However, Rowling's role is not without its challenges, as her presence also brings a degree of controversy that HBO must navigate delicately.

Balancing Act: Her Creative Insights vs. Public Backlash

Rowling's creative involvement in the series is accompanied by significant public scrutiny, largely stemming from her outspoken views on transgender issues. Since 2019, Rowling has faced widespread criticism for statements that many consider transphobic, sparking boycotts and protests from both fans and LGBTQ+ advocacy groups. This controversy presents a complex challenge for HBO: while Rowling's creative insights are invaluable, her polarizing public persona has the potential to overshadow the series.

The network has taken a measured approach in addressing this dynamic. In official statements, HBO has emphasized Rowling's right to express her personal views while focusing on her contributions as a storyteller. This careful framing aims to separate her creative legacy from her personal opinions, allowing the series to move forward without alienating its diverse audience.

At the same time, HBO has doubled down on its commitment to inclusivity. The open casting call for the series explicitly highlighted the network's dedication to diversity, inviting actors of all ethnicities, genders, and abilities to audition for key roles. This inclusive approach serves as a counterbalance to the controversies surrounding Rowling, signaling to fans that the show is a progressive reimagining of the wizarding world.

For Rowling, the backlash has also been an opportunity to clarify her position. She has described herself as a "left-leaning liberal fiercely opposed to authoritarianism" and has defended her views as rooted in concerns for women's rights. However, her comments continue to polarize audiences, with some fans choosing to distance themselves from the franchise altogether. Despite this, Rowling remains steadfast in her creative vision, working closely with HBO to ensure that the series remains faithful to the books.

The balancing act between leveraging Rowling's creative insights and addressing the public backlash is a delicate one. It underscores the broader tension between honoring the past and embracing the future—a theme that resonates not only in the series but also in its production journey.

A Longstanding Partnership: Rowling and HBO's Two-Decade Collaboration

Rowling's relationship with HBO and its parent company, Warner Bros., spans over two decades, beginning with the adaptation of "Harry Potter and the Sorcerer's Stone" in 2001. This long-standing partnership has been characterized by mutual respect and a shared commitment to bringing the wizarding world to life with unparalleled quality and authenticity.

From the outset, Warner Bros. recognized the cultural significance of Rowling's work and prioritized her involvement in the filmmaking process. Unlike many authors who relinquish creative control during adaptations, Rowling maintained an active role in key decisions, from approving scripts to overseeing casting choices. Her insistence on filming in the UK, using British actors, and preserving the essence of the books ensured that the films remained true to her vision.

This collaborative dynamic laid the foundation for the success of the original "Harry Potter" films, which collectively grossed over $7.7 billion worldwide. It also established a precedent for Rowling's involvement in subsequent projects, including the "Fantastic Beasts" films and the stage production of "Harry Potter and the Cursed Child."

HBO's decision to bring Rowling on board as an executive producer for the television series is a natural extension of this partnership. Over the years, the network has demonstrated its ability to adapt complex narratives into critically acclaimed series, from "Game of Thrones" to "The Last of Us." By combining Rowling's storytelling expertise with HBO's production prowess, the two entities aim to create a series that surpasses the expectations of even the most devoted fans.

However, this collaboration is not without its challenges. The media landscape has evolved significantly since the release of the original films, and audiences now expect greater inclusivity, representation, and sensitivity in storytelling. HBO's partnership with Rowling must navigate these changing dynamics while preserving the core elements that made "Harry Potter" a global phenomenon.

As the series moves into production, the enduring partnership between Rowling and HBO stands as a testament to the power of collaboration. Together, they have shaped the cultural legacy of "Harry Potter," and their continued efforts promise to redefine the magical world for a new generation.

CHAPTER THREE

Casting Harry, Ron, and Hermione for a New Era

The casting process for HBO's "Harry Potter" series has been one of the most anticipated aspects of the production. In September 2023, HBO announced an open casting call for the lead roles of Harry, Ron, and Hermione, signaling the beginning of a meticulous search for the new faces of these iconic characters.

The casting call emphasized the network's commitment to inclusivity, welcoming actors of all ethnicities, genders, and abilities to audition. This progressive approach represents a significant shift from the original films, which featured a predominantly white cast.

HBO's emphasis on diversity aligns with broader trends in the entertainment industry, where representation has become a central focus. The network has been clear that its goal is to find actors who not only embody the spirit of the characters but also bring fresh perspectives to the roles. This decision to prioritize talent and interpretation over adherence to physical descriptions from the books underscores HBO's commitment to modernizing the franchise.

The inclusive casting approach also reflects the global appeal of "Harry Potter." With fans spanning continents, languages, and cultures, the series has an unparalleled opportunity to embrace diversity and create a cast that resonates with a worldwide audience. For many, seeing characters like Hermione or Ron portrayed by actors of different ethnic backgrounds would not only be a refreshing change but also a step toward making the wizarding world feel more accessible and inclusive.

HBO's process has been thorough, with the network reportedly fielding thousands of auditions from aspiring actors worldwide. Casting directors have been tasked with finding performers who can balance the complexity of these roles—capturing the innocence, growth, and resilience of the trio while honoring the essence of Rowling's characters. By taking an open-minded and inclusive approach, HBO has set the stage for a casting process that could redefine how fans view these beloved characters.

Challenges and Expectations: Filling Iconic Roles

Filling the roles of Harry, Ron, and Hermione is no easy feat. These characters are not just central to the story—they are cultural icons who have defined an entire generation's relationship with the "Harry Potter" franchise. The challenge lies in finding actors who can live up to the monumental expectations set by both fans and the legacy of the original films.

One of the most significant hurdles is the inevitable comparison to Daniel Radcliffe, Rupert Grint, and Emma Watson, whose portrayals of the trio are etched into the collective consciousness of fans worldwide. The original actors brought charm, depth, and relatability to their roles, creating a standard that new performers will have to meet—or surpass.

Another challenge lies in capturing the unique dynamics of the Golden Trio. Harry's quiet bravery, Ron's unwavering loyalty, and Hermione's fierce intellect form the heart of the story, and any misstep in casting could disrupt the delicate balance of these relationships. Casting directors must find actors who not only excel individually but also share an undeniable chemistry as a group.

Age-appropriate casting is another critical factor. The original films famously cast young, relatively unknown actors in the lead roles, allowing audiences to watch them grow alongside their characters. HBO appears to be following a similar strategy, searching for young talent who can authentically portray the trio's evolution from wide-eyed first-years to battle-hardened heroes.

Finally, the weight of fan expectations adds an extra layer of pressure. With millions of fans eagerly awaiting the casting announcements, any decision is bound to spark debate. Whether it's discussions about physical resemblance to the book descriptions or the actors' perceived ability to handle the emotional depth of the roles, the scrutiny will be intense. For HBO, the key lies in staying true to the spirit of the characters while embracing the fresh possibilities offered by a new cast.

Fan Reactions: Enthusiasm and Skepticism About Diverse Casting

The decision to pursue diverse casting for Harry, Ron, and Hermione has sparked a wave of reactions from fans, ranging from enthusiastic support to cautious skepticism. For many, the announcement represents a welcome step toward modernizing the "Harry Potter" series and making it more reflective of the world's diversity.

Supporters of the move argue that the original books' themes—acceptance, courage, and unity—naturally lend themselves to an inclusive interpretation. They see diverse casting as an opportunity to expand the boundaries of representation within the wizarding world, creating a richer and more relatable narrative for contemporary audiences.

Social media platforms have been flooded with fan art and casting suggestions that imagine the trio as actors of different ethnicities, genders, and cultural backgrounds, showcasing the excitement and creativity sparked by the prospect of diverse casting.

However, not all fans are on board. Some have expressed concerns about deviating too far from the characters' descriptions in the books, fearing that it might disrupt their connection to the story. Others worry that the emphasis on diversity could feel performative or detract from the series' focus on storytelling. This skepticism reflects a broader tension in fandoms between honoring the source material and adapting it for modern sensibilities.

Additionally, the controversy surrounding J.K. Rowling's views has further complicated fan reactions. While some fans are eager to see how the series might address issues of inclusivity, others remain wary of supporting a project so closely tied to Rowling's creative control. This divide has led to nuanced discussions about how the series can reconcile its progressive goals with the legacy of its creator.

Despite the mixed reactions, one thing is clear: the casting decisions for Harry, Ron, and Hermione will be a defining moment for the series. Whether the choices ignite widespread enthusiasm or fuel further debate, they will set the tone for the show's reception and its place within the broader "Harry Potter" legacy. For HBO, navigating these complexities with care and thoughtfulness will be essential to ensuring that the magic of the series resonates with old and new fans alike.

CHAPTER FOUR

Controversies and Conversations Around Inclusivity

J.K. Rowling's outspoken views on gender and transgender rights have had a profound and polarizing impact on the "Harry Potter" fandom and broader cultural discourse. Since 2019, when Rowling publicly supported Maya Forstater, a researcher who lost her job over her views on biological sex, the author has become a lightning rod for debates about gender identity.

Her essay in June 2020, in which she expressed concerns about "trans activism" and its implications for women's rights, further deepened the divide.

For many fans, Rowling's comments are seen as antithetical to the values of inclusivity and acceptance central to the "Harry Potter" series. The wizarding world she created is often viewed as a metaphorical safe haven for outsiders, marginalized groups, and those who feel different—a vision that has resonated with LGBTQ+ individuals and communities worldwide. Rowling's statements have, in the eyes of some, betrayed the very ideals her work inspired, leading to widespread backlash and boycotts.

The impact on the fandom has been profound. Social media platforms like Twitter and Tumblr, once vibrant spaces for "Harry Potter" enthusiasts, have become battlegrounds for heated debates about the series and its creator. Many fans have chosen to distance themselves from Rowling while still cherishing the books and movies as cultural artifacts. Others have reimagined the wizarding world through fan fiction and fan art, deliberately creating inclusive narratives that challenge the perceived limitations of Rowling's vision.

At the same time, Rowling has retained a vocal and loyal base of supporters. These individuals defend her right to free speech and view her comments as legitimate concerns about preserving women's spaces. This faction argues that separating art from the artist is essential, pointing out that Rowling's creative contributions to literature and film should not be overshadowed by her personal opinions.

Rowling's views have also reverberated beyond the "Harry Potter" fandom, influencing broader discussions about the responsibilities of creators, the limits of free expression, and the complexities of cancel culture. As HBO embarks on its adaptation, it faces the challenge of balancing Rowling's indispensable creative role with the need to address the sensitivities of modern audiences.

HBO's Commitment to Diversity: Navigating Public Criticism

HBO has made a concerted effort to position its "Harry Potter" series as a fresh and inclusive reimagining of the beloved story. The network's casting call, which explicitly encouraged actors of diverse ethnicities, genders, and abilities to audition, reflects its commitment to representation. This progressive stance marks a departure from the original films, which, while groundbreaking in their storytelling, were critiqued for their lack of diversity.

However, HBO's efforts have not been immune to criticism. Skeptics argue that the network's diversity initiatives may be perceived as performative or an attempt to offset the controversies surrounding Rowling. For these critics, the challenge lies in ensuring that inclusivity is woven seamlessly into the fabric of the series rather than appearing as a superficial add-on.

HBO's leadership has acknowledged the tightrope it must walk. In statements to the press, executives have emphasized the importance of honoring the original story while updating it to reflect contemporary values. This approach includes not only diverse casting but also a broader commitment to telling stories that resonate with audiences of all backgrounds. For example, the series has the potential to explore themes of identity, belonging, and resistance in ways that feel especially relevant in today's social and political climate.

The network's stance has garnered praise from many fans and industry observers. By prioritizing inclusivity, HBO signals its willingness to evolve the "Harry Potter" franchise while preserving the magic that made it a cultural phenomenon. Still, the network must contend with the challenge of meeting high expectations from fans who view the series as a litmus test for how well the entertainment industry can balance tradition and progress.

The Broader Cultural Landscape: Gender Identity in Media Today

The "Harry Potter" series is being developed during a time of heightened awareness and debate about gender identity in media and society. Transgender and nonbinary representation in film and television has become a focal point for discussions about inclusivity, with advocates pushing for greater visibility and authenticity in storytelling. Against this backdrop, HBO's adaptation of "Harry Potter" is uniquely positioned to contribute to the conversation.

Over the past decade, the entertainment industry has made strides toward better representation of LGBTQ+ characters and narratives. Shows like "Pose," "Euphoria," and "The Umbrella Academy" have introduced complex, multidimensional portrayals of gender-diverse characters, challenging stereotypes and broadening the scope of mainstream storytelling.

These shifts have been accompanied by calls for increased opportunities for transgender and nonbinary actors, writers, and directors, ensuring that their stories are told with authenticity and nuance.

HBO's commitment to diversity offers an opportunity to engage with these trends. The wizarding world, with its rich lore and allegorical potential, provides fertile ground for exploring themes of identity and transformation. Whether it's through introducing new characters, reinterpreting existing ones, or addressing societal issues metaphorically, the series has the potential to make meaningful contributions to the broader cultural discourse.

However, this opportunity comes with significant challenges. As debates about gender identity become increasingly polarized, the series risks becoming a lightning rod for criticism from all sides. Some viewers may resist any perceived departures from the original story, while others may demand bolder, more explicit representations of LGBTQ+ experiences. Striking the right balance will require careful storytelling and a willingness to engage with audiences thoughtfully and authentically.

In this context, HBO's "Harry Potter" series is more than just an adaptation—it is a reflection of the cultural moment in which it is being created. By embracing inclusivity and engaging with the complexities of gender identity, the series has the potential to redefine the wizarding world for a new generation while contributing to the ongoing evolution of representation in media.

CHAPTER FIVE

Crafting a Faithful Adaptation

One of the most prominent promises surrounding HBO's "Harry Potter" series is its commitment to being a "faithful adaptation" of J.K. Rowling's original books. This pledge comes as a direct response to both long-time fans who want a deeper exploration of the novels' intricate world-building and critics who felt the original films left out critical elements of the story.

The books' rich narrative, spanning over 4,000 pages, features an array of subplots, characters, and world-building details that were inevitably compressed or omitted in the film adaptations.

From the complexities of characters like Peeves the Poltergeist, Winky the house-elf, and the deeply layered backstory of Tom Riddle, there is a wealth of material waiting to be brought to life on screen. For many fans, these omissions left gaps in the cinematic experience, and HBO's new adaptation offers a chance to fill those gaps and present a fuller picture of Rowling's wizarding world.

Authenticity also extends to the tone and themes of the books. While the films largely maintained the story's magical allure, some argue that they leaned heavily into action-adventure elements, occasionally at the expense of the books' subtler emotional beats. HBO has the opportunity to dive deeper into the internal struggles of its characters, their moral dilemmas, and the philosophical questions posed by the series—such as the nature of good and evil, the value of sacrifice, and the importance of choice in shaping one's destiny.

However, staying true to the books is not without its challenges. Rowling's detailed descriptions of the wizarding world come with a level of specificity that can be daunting to translate into live-action. From Hogwarts' ever-changing staircases to the intricacies of Quidditch matches, the visual demands of the series will require a combination of practical effects and cutting-edge CGI. Additionally, certain elements that worked well in text—such as Rowling's wordplay or the inner monologues of her characters—will need creative reinterpretation to resonate on screen.

For fans, the promise of authenticity is both a reassurance and an expectation. By committing to a faithful adaptation, HBO is not only embracing the essence of the source material but also setting a high bar for itself. The success of the series will depend on its ability to honor the books while using the medium of television to enhance and expand upon the storytelling.

Revisiting Key Themes: Friendship, Courage, and Acceptance

At its core, "Harry Potter" is a story about friendship, courage, and acceptance—universal themes that have resonated with readers for decades. As HBO revisits the series, these themes will remain central to its narrative, serving as the emotional foundation for the show.

"Friendship" lies at the heart of the series, particularly through the bond between Harry, Ron, and Hermione. Their relationship, marked by loyalty, occasional conflicts, and unwavering support, is a driving force behind the story's most pivotal moments.

The series will have the opportunity to delve even deeper into their dynamic, exploring not only their triumphs but also the challenges they face as they grow and change. From Hermione's struggle to reconcile her Muggle-born identity with her place in the wizarding world to Ron's insecurities about living in Harry's shadow, these nuances can be given more room to breathe in a long-form adaptation.

"Courage" is another key theme, embodied by Harry's journey from an orphaned boy living under the stairs to a leader who defies insurmountable odds. HBO's adaptation can explore the many forms that courage takes in the story—from Neville Longbottom's quiet bravery to Dobby's selfless acts of defiance. By emphasizing these moments, the series can underscore the idea that heroism is not confined to grand gestures but is also found in everyday acts of resistance and kindness.

"Acceptance" is perhaps the most poignant theme, woven throughout the narrative in various ways. The series tackles prejudice and discrimination through the lens of the wizarding world, addressing issues like blood purity, house-elf enslavement, and societal biases. These parallels to real-world issues have made the series a source of comfort and inspiration for marginalized communities.

The HBO adaptation has the potential to highlight these themes with even greater depth, using its expanded runtime to explore how characters like Hermione, Lupin, and even Snape navigate the challenges of acceptance.

By revisiting these themes, the new adaptation can recapture the magic of the original story while offering fresh insights for contemporary audiences. These universal messages, combined with the series' fantastical elements, ensure that "Harry Potter" will continue to resonate across generations.

Adapting for the Screen: Challenges of Long-Form Storytelling

While a seven-season format offers unparalleled opportunities for in-depth storytelling, it also comes with unique challenges. The episodic nature of television requires careful pacing, balancing the need for standalone arcs with the overarching narrative of each season.

One of the most significant challenges is the series' structure. Each book will reportedly serve as the basis for one season, but this raises questions about how the show will handle the varying lengths and tones of the novels. For instance, the brevity of "The Philosopher's Stone" contrasts sharply with the complexity of "The Order of the Phoenix." Translating these differences into cohesive seasons will require thoughtful adaptation to ensure that each story feels complete while maintaining momentum across the series.

Another challenge lies in maintaining consistency over the show's long run. With a cast that will age alongside their characters, production schedules will need to account for the natural growth of the actors. This adds a layer of logistical complexity, as the series must balance the demands of filming with the personal development of its young cast. The show's creators will also need to plan for the evolving dynamics of the story, ensuring that character arcs and relationships remain compelling throughout the seven-season journey.

Visual effects are another critical consideration. The magical elements of the story—from spellcasting to mythical creatures—require a level of realism that can be difficult to achieve on a television budget. However, advancements in CGI and practical effects offer new possibilities for bringing the wizarding world to life in ways that were not possible during the original films.

Finally, the series must navigate audience expectations. Long-form storytelling allows for a deeper exploration of the books' subplots and secondary characters, but it also requires striking a balance between faithfulness to the source material and creative innovation. Fans will expect iconic moments to be handled with care while also hoping for surprises that enhance their understanding of the story.

Despite these challenges, the long-form format is an exciting opportunity to reimagine "Harry Potter" for television. By embracing the medium's strengths—its capacity for character development, world-building, and nuanced storytelling—HBO can create a series that not only honors the original books but also elevates them to new heights.

The Complete Inside Story of HBO's Most Anticipated Show

CHAPTER SIX

The Creative Team Behind the Magic

The Harry Potter series' success is often attributed to the collaborative efforts of a creative team that included visionary writers, directors, and producers. As HBO embarks on adapting J.K. Rowling's iconic books for television, the network has emphasized the importance of selecting a creative team that can stay true to the original while bringing new dimensions to the story.

Rowling's involvement in handpicking key members of the creative team underscores the importance of maintaining the integrity of the original work while ensuring that the series meets modern standards of storytelling.

Writers and directors play a critical role in translating the magic of the wizarding world onto the screen. Their job is not only to craft a compelling narrative but also to respect the essence of the characters and world-building that made Harry Potter a cultural phenomenon.

HBO has made clear that Rowling is deeply involved in the selection process for both writers and directors, ensuring that her voice and vision are preserved in this adaptation. However, it's also important that the directors and writers bring fresh perspectives, especially considering the vast, multi-season format and the need for continuity across a lengthy production.

HBO's careful selection process aims to bring on board experienced individuals who have a deep understanding of fantasy and magical realism, as well as the unique challenges of adapting a beloved literary franchise for the screen. Additionally, the team must balance the original material with new creative contributions, ensuring that the series resonates with a contemporary audience while honoring the spirit of the books. By tapping into a pool of diverse talent, HBO hopes to create a show that is both familiar and innovative.

In terms of directing, the challenge will be to capture the broad emotional range of the

Harry Potter saga—from moments of lighthearted humor and youthful adventure to darker, more dramatic storylines. The directors selected will need to work closely with the writers to ensure the series flows smoothly over multiple seasons, creating a narrative that is both episodic and cohesive.

Collaborating with Original Film Talent: A Legacy Connection

While the HBO adaptation is forging its own creative path, the series cannot ignore the profound legacy left by the original Harry Potter films. These films set a high standard for adapting Rowling's world to the screen and created an iconic cinematic universe that continues to influence pop culture. To ensure the series feels like an extension of that universe, HBO is likely to seek collaboration with some of the original talent who contributed to the films.

For example, the film's iconic production designer, Stuart Craig, who helped bring Hogwarts and its surrounding magical world to life, could provide invaluable input in the reimagining of these locations for the television series. Similarly, veteran composer John Williams' score remains one of the most beloved aspects of the films. While the series will undoubtedly have a new musical direction, there may be an effort to incorporate elements of Williams' iconic compositions or collaborate with new composers who respect the franchise's musical legacy.

Additionally, some of the original film's producers, cinematographers, or visual effects artists may be invited to consult on the series to ensure that the magic of the wizarding world is preserved. Such collaborations would bridge the gap between the world of the films and the new direction of the TV adaptation, ensuring continuity while embracing new storytelling techniques.

However, the involvement of original film talent is a double-edged sword. While their expertise could help anchor the new series in the visual language that fans know and love, the creative team must avoid falling into the trap of simply mimicking what has been done before. Instead, they must use the legacy of the films as a foundation upon which to build something fresh and engaging for a new generation of viewers.

New Faces, Fresh Perspectives: The Producers' Vision

As much as HBO is leaning on the expertise of veteran creators and maintaining a connection to the original films, the network is also committed to bringing fresh perspectives into the creative process. This involves assembling a team of producers, writers, and directors who are new to the Harry Potter universe but can still bring a modern sensibility to the project.

In particular, the producers play an essential role in shaping the tone and direction of the series. Their ability to balance the old and the new will be key to how the series resonates with both loyal fans and new viewers. With the increasing demand for more diverse and socially conscious storytelling, producers will likely face pressure to introduce more inclusive narratives while still adhering to the themes of friendship, loyalty, and bravery that defined the original books.

Many of the producers likely come from a background in fantasy television, with experience in shows like Game of Thrones or His Dark Materials. These shows, much like Harry Potter, combine rich world-building with intense character-driven drama. Such experience will be crucial for ensuring that the show can handle the narrative depth required for a seven-season series.

The producers will also have to juggle the demands of long-form television—managing multiple seasons, tracking character arcs over many years, and maintaining audience interest without losing the show's integrity.

One of the key challenges for the producers is to push the boundaries of the wizarding world while staying faithful to the essence of the original work. For instance, the series will have the opportunity to explore untold stories from the books, delve deeper into secondary characters, and explore social and political dynamics within the wizarding world.

These expansions will require innovative thinking and the ability to tell a compelling story over an extended period of time. The producers will have to ensure that these elements complement the established Harry Potter universe, rather than overshadowing or disrupting it.

Finally, as part of the production team, the executive producers are likely to be the linchpins of the entire operation, guiding both the creative and logistical aspects of the series. Their ability to maintain cohesion across the multiple seasons, ensuring consistency in tone, character development, and thematic resonance, will be vital for the series' long-term success.

Overall, the creative team behind HBO's Harry Potter series is a blend of experienced talent from the original films and fresh faces with new perspectives on the world of magic. The collaboration between these two groups will play a significant role in shaping the series, creating an adaptation that honors its legacy while also introducing new dimensions that keep the franchise exciting for a new generation.

CHAPTER SEVEN

Production Design and World-Building

One of the most crucial elements of adapting Harry Potter to television is the task of reimagining the world that has become synonymous with magic, mystery, and adventure—Hogwarts School of Witchcraft and Wizardry.

For long-time fans, Hogwarts is not just a setting but a character in itself: its towering spires, the endless moving staircases, the enchanted ceiling of the Great Hall, and its sprawling grounds have etched themselves into the collective memory of a generation. Recreating this world while ensuring it feels both familiar and new is a monumental challenge for the Harry Potter series.

The key challenge for HBO will be in balancing the nostalgic elements that fans have come to expect with fresh visual interpretations that update the world for a new era of viewers. The castle itself, a sprawling, labyrinthine fortress, will need to retain its iconic features—the towering turrets, the enchanted doors, the grand hallways—while offering new insights into its inner workings.

The Great Hall, for example, may retain its grandeur but be enhanced with even more magical elements, such as animated tapestries or more elaborate feast scenes, providing the depth and richness that long-form television can afford.

Hogwarts will also need to reflect the passage of time. While the films presented a version of the castle that was largely timeless, the TV series has the potential to explore how the school evolves over the years, integrating both a sense of history and the presence of new magical innovations.

As the series progresses, we may see how the wizarding world's political shifts, cultural trends, and technological advancements impact the design and function of Hogwarts. For instance, new magical classrooms could be introduced, or the architecture could be re-imagined to reflect certain themes explored in later seasons of the show, like the rise of new powers and factions.

Beyond Hogwarts itself, the world-building extends to the broader magical community, including the various magical shops in Diagon Alley, the ministry buildings of the Ministry of Magic, and the Wizarding World's hidden locations like the Forbidden Forest and Hagrid's hut. While these places have already been established in the films, the television format provides more time to explore these spaces in greater detail.

More in-depth designs could delve into the hidden nooks of Diagon Alley or the dark, magical corners of the Forbidden Forest, giving fans an immersive look into areas that were only briefly glimpsed in the past.

Ultimately, the challenge for the production designers will be to reimagine these iconic locations in a way that preserves their magic and mystery, while inviting new interpretations that expand the world for both long-time fans and newcomers to the franchise.

Special Effects in a New Era: Advancements in Technology

When the Harry Potter films were first made, the use of special effects was cutting-edge, with the filmmakers relying heavily on practical effects combined with groundbreaking CGI. However, as technology has advanced significantly since the release of the last film, HBO's new Harry Potter series will benefit from even more sophisticated tools that can bring the wizarding world to life in new and exciting ways.

One area where advancements in technology will play a significant role is in the realm of magical creatures and beasts. From Hippogriffs to dragons, the magical creatures of the Harry Potter universe are essential to the world-building of the series.

With the new special effects technologies available, creatures can be brought to life with more realistic animations, giving them more personality and realism than ever before. Motion capture and CGI techniques, which have evolved dramatically since the original films, will allow these creatures to be integrated seamlessly into live-action scenes, making them feel as though they inhabit the same world as the human characters.

In addition to magical creatures, the advancement of special effects will allow for even more intricate spell-casting. The films showcased dazzling visual effects for spells like the iconic "Expelliarmus" and "Expecto Patronum." The television format allows for more time to showcase spell-casting in a variety of creative ways, and with improved technology, the spells may appear even more detailed and dynamic.

For example, a scene involving a duel between two wizards could explore how spells interact with their environment in ways that go beyond what was possible in the films, creating breathtaking visuals that draw viewers deeper into the action.

Additionally, modern special effects allow for a more seamless blend of practical and digital effects. For instance, while the films used green screens and practical sets, newer technologies such as virtual production—used in projects like The Mandalorian—could offer the possibility of building entire magical worlds on LED soundstages, where actors can interact with their environment in real-time. This technology allows for a more immersive and responsive set, where the physical and digital elements of a scene coexist harmoniously.

The television series also has the luxury of time to elaborate on magical systems and concepts in ways that the films did not. With the ability to produce a multi-season show, the effects team will have more freedom to explore how magic works, showcasing new and more complex magical phenomena that were not previously possible. From more elaborate Transfiguration spells to new enchanted objects, the expanding use of special effects in the series will be essential in conveying the full breadth and depth of the magical world.

Costume and Set Design: Evoking Magic Through Detail

Another vital aspect of building the Harry Potter world for television is the costume and set design. The wardrobe and sets of the original films became iconic in their own right, from the students' robes to the magical artifacts scattered throughout the wizarding world. HBO will be tasked with reimagining these elements, ensuring they stay true to the books while simultaneously bringing them into the modern era.

Costume design plays a key role in signaling the passage of time, status, and the unique qualities of each character. While the original films primarily focused on the robes of Hogwarts students and the iconic attire of key characters like Harry, Hermione, and Ron, the TV series will have the chance to explore the clothing in greater detail, reflecting not only personal style but also the socioeconomic and cultural divisions in the wizarding world.

The varied houses at Hogwarts, for example, could have distinct sartorial identities that reflect their values and histories. The costumes will also need to reflect changes in character development. For instance, the transformation of Harry from a young boy into a young adult will likely be mirrored by the evolution of his wardrobe, moving from his ill-fitting clothes to the more mature and tailored robes he might wear in later seasons.

Additionally, the set design will need to balance practicality with the fantasy elements that define the series. Hogwarts itself, with its enormous, mysterious corridors and hidden spaces, will require a set design that blends the magic of the world with the realism needed to make the environment feel lived-in and believable.

The Great Hall, for instance, must evoke the grandeur and warmth that has become synonymous with the school, while the common rooms for each house will need to feel distinct and reflective of the students who inhabit them.

Set designers will also have the opportunity to explore the broader wizarding world. Places like Diagon Alley, Hagrid's hut, and the Ministry of Magic will be given new life with careful attention to detail. The visual cues that made these places memorable in the films—such as the quirky storefronts of Diagon Alley or the dark, looming corridors of the Ministry—will be recreated and expanded upon in the series. This may involve deeper exploration of the magical spaces that were previously only briefly explored or glimpsed in the original films.

Overall, the costume and set design will be fundamental in establishing the immersive quality of the show, ensuring that the magic of Harry Potter is conveyed through every stitch of clothing and every detail of the environments. The goal will be to evoke the same sense of wonder and excitement that fans felt when first introduced to Rowling's world, while also offering new interpretations that keep the series visually fresh and dynamic.

CHAPTER EIGHT

Fan Reactions and Divided Opinions

As one of the most beloved and influential franchises in modern literature and cinema, the Harry Potter universe has cultivated a passionate and diverse global fanbase. Potterheads, as the fans are known, have an intense attachment to the series, from the books to the films to the broader cultural phenomenon that the wizarding world has become.

With the announcement of the new HBO Harry Potter television series, fans have expressed a wide range of emotions, from enthusiastic excitement about the prospect of revisiting the magical world, to deep concern regarding potential changes to the beloved story or the involvement of author J.K. Rowling.

On one hand, many fans are elated by the prospect of a more faithful adaptation of the books. The films, while successful and beloved, were inevitably limited by time constraints, which resulted in the exclusion or alteration of key scenes and details that fans cherished in the books.

With the promise of a seven-season series, there is a sense of anticipation among fans that they will be able to witness their favorite moments in full, such as the exploration of minor characters like Peeves the Poltergeist, or the detailed exploration of the wizarding world beyond Hogwarts.

For some, the television series is an opportunity to revisit the original magic that drew them to the books in the first place. The prospect of seeing Harry, Ron, Hermione, and their peers grow over multiple seasons, as well as seeing the intricate relationships and conflicts that unfold over a longer period of time, has generated significant excitement among fans who longed for more Harry Potter content.

There's also anticipation around the world-building possibilities, including the deeper exploration of the various magical institutions, creatures, and histories that were only briefly touched upon in the films.

On the other hand, a vocal portion of the fanbase is concerned about what the new series will mean for the legacy of Harry Potter. For some, the involvement of J.K. Rowling as an executive producer has raised concerns, particularly given her controversial views on transgender issues.

Critics argue that her stance could overshadow the story's positive messages of acceptance, tolerance, and friendship, which are central to the Harry Potter ethos. These fans fear that the series may become too closely associated with her personal beliefs, potentially alienating marginalized groups or perpetuating harmful stereotypes.

Additionally, some long-time fans express wariness about the casting process. The announcement of a more inclusive, diverse approach to casting has sparked both excitement and anxiety. While many fans are hopeful that the show will reflect the changing times and offer representation to groups that were previously underrepresented, others worry about the potential for "wokeness" to overshadow the original story.

They fear that efforts to diversify the cast could be seen as tokenism or could undermine the authenticity of the world-building, particularly if characters are changed in a way that they believe contradicts the original text.

Ultimately, the emotional divide among Potterheads reflects a broader tension between nostalgia for the original Harry Potter films and the desire for a new, more inclusive vision. While many fans eagerly anticipate the new series, others are deeply skeptical, and the show's ability to bridge these divergent opinions will be key to its success.

Online Backlash: The Role of Social Media in Shaping Perceptions

The rise of social media has transformed the way fans engage with media and franchises. In the past, fan reactions to new adaptations or announcements could be contained within communities or fan conventions. Today, however, social media platforms such as Twitter (now X), Instagram, and TikTok provide fans with direct channels to voice their opinions, share their thoughts, and spark debates—often at lightning speed.

When it comes to the Harry Potter television series, social media has played an instrumental role in shaping the discourse. On the one hand, there has been an outpouring of support for the show, with fans expressing excitement about the opportunity to revisit the wizarding world. Hashtags like #Potterhead and #HarryPotterSeries have filled timelines with positive posts, fan art, and speculation about the direction of the new show.

Many fans have used social media to connect with like-minded individuals who share their enthusiasm, and these platforms have become a space where speculation and anticipation are built.

On the other hand, social media has also become a platform for backlash and criticism. The ongoing controversy surrounding J.K. Rowling's views on transgender issues has led to widespread discussions on platforms like Twitter, where many people have openly criticized the author's involvement in the project.

Some fans, activists, and even members of the LGBTQ+ community have used social media to voice their opposition, calling for boycotts of the show or urging the production team to reconsider Rowling's role as executive producer. These debates have been heated, with some fans taking to social media to call for greater inclusion and diversity in the series, while others defend Rowling's right to hold and express her opinions.

The speed and intensity of online backlash can amplify criticism and create a sense of division within the fanbase. As opinions on the new series become increasingly polarized, the pressure on HBO to address these concerns grows. Social media campaigns can quickly influence public perception, and how the network responds to the criticism will be important in determining the show's reception. The show's messaging, public relations efforts, and its handling of controversies will all be scrutinized, and social media will likely continue to play a central role in shaping the narrative around the series.

Importantly, the backlash also raises questions about the influence of social media on mainstream media and entertainment. Fans can now directly engage with producers, writers, and creators in ways that were previously impossible. The instant feedback loop created by platforms like Twitter and Instagram means that the success or failure of a major series can be determined not just by traditional reviews, but also by online sentiment. As such, HBO's handling of fan reactions will be critical to the show's ongoing relevance and longevity.

Balancing Legacy and Progress: The Show's Responsibility

One of the central challenges of the Harry Potter series adaptation lies in finding the balance between honoring the legacy of the original books and films while also moving the story forward to reflect contemporary social dynamics. The world of Harry Potter has always been rooted in themes of friendship, love, and acceptance, and the show carries the responsibility of staying true to these messages while addressing the concerns of an increasingly diverse and socially conscious audience.

The show's responsibility goes beyond simply adapting the books to the screen; it also includes navigating the changing cultural landscape. As society becomes more aware of issues related to race, gender, and identity, the Harry Potter series will need to engage with these themes in a sensitive and thoughtful manner. This responsibility includes reimagining certain aspects of the books to reflect the values of today's viewers, such as updating the representation of marginalized communities, particularly in terms of gender, race, and sexual orientation.

The series has the opportunity to break new ground by providing greater visibility to characters and communities that were underrepresented in the original films, ensuring that the wizarding world feels inclusive and welcoming to all.

At the same time, there is a strong desire among fans for the series to maintain the essence of the original Harry Potter world. The characters, the magic, the relationships, and the overarching storylines are beloved, and any deviation from this formula risks alienating long-time fans. Striking the right balance between honoring the legacy of Harry Potter while pushing forward with progress on representation and inclusion is a delicate task that will be central to the success of the series.

The show's creators must also consider how to navigate the complexities of J.K. Rowling's involvement in the project. While Rowling's personal views have caused controversy, her work remains at the core of the Harry Potter franchise.

The show has a responsibility to maintain the values of friendship, courage, and acceptance that are central to her books, while distancing itself from views that may undermine those messages. How the series addresses the growing calls for inclusivity, while also dealing with the legacy of the author's statements, will be critical in determining the series' cultural relevance and success.

Ultimately, the Harry Potter series has a unique responsibility to its fans, the broader cultural landscape, and its own legacy. By balancing these factors with care and thoughtfulness, the show has the potential to become a landmark in television, both as an adaptation of a beloved work and as a conversation starter about inclusion, identity, and the changing landscape of media.

CHAPTER NINE

Industry Implications and HBO's High Stakes

As streaming services continue to vie for dominance in an increasingly crowded market, content is king. The rise of platforms like Netflix, Disney+, Amazon Prime, and Hulu has prompted traditional media giants to accelerate their own offerings, and franchises like Harry Potter are an essential piece of this content-driven arms race.

HBO's decision to adapt the Harry Potter books into a high-budget, seven-season series is not just an artistic endeavor—it's a calculated business strategy aimed at securing a competitive advantage in the ongoing streaming wars.

The success of the Harry Potter television series could help solidify HBO Max's position as a dominant force in the streaming space. By leveraging the massive global fanbase and cultural cache of the Harry Potter franchise, HBO aims to attract millions of subscribers, not only from existing fans but also from a younger generation who may not have grown up with the films or the books.

Franchise-based adaptations like this one are highly coveted because they provide a built-in audience, ensuring that the show enters the market with a strong viewership base.

Moreover, the Harry Potter franchise has significant cross-platform potential. The series can be marketed not just as a television show, but as part of a larger wizarding world ecosystem, encompassing video games, theme park attractions, merchandise, and more.

This integration allows HBO to tap into a vast revenue stream while strengthening its brand as a purveyor of premium, iconic content. Much like Disney's approach with Star Wars and Marvel, HBO's bet on Harry Potter is about creating a sprawling, interconnected experience that keeps subscribers engaged across multiple mediums.

However, as HBO continues to compete with other streaming services, the Harry Potter series will not exist in a vacuum. The market is flooded with adaptations of beloved IPs, and HBO will need to ensure that their interpretation of Harry Potter stands out in an oversaturated market.

They must balance the nostalgia and fan expectations with a fresh vision that appeals to both long-time enthusiasts and new viewers. The success of this series will set a precedent for how HBO handles future franchise adaptations, signaling whether their high-risk, high-reward strategy pays off or if the pressure to produce hit content will backfire.

Financial and Cultural Investments: What's on the Line for HBO

The financial investment in a Harry Potter television series is staggering. It is one of the most significant commitments in the history of HBO Max, with multi-million-dollar budgets allocated to ensure the show lives up to the grandeur of the films while delivering the long-form storytelling expected of a high-profile series.

Beyond the high production costs, which include elaborate sets, cutting-edge special effects, and an all-star cast, HBO also faces the risk of alienating potential subscribers if the show fails to meet expectations. For HBO, the Harry Potter series represents a bet on its future in the streaming market—a high-stakes project that has the potential to both fuel growth and define the network's long-term success.

From a financial standpoint, Harry Potter holds immense potential. The franchise's past box-office successes and the continued popularity of the films and related media mean that HBO can reasonably expect strong viewership. However, the pressure to produce a hit is immense, particularly with the significant investment involved.

The series is expected to span seven seasons, and the production value required to maintain the grandeur of the wizarding world will need to be sustained throughout this long commitment. This type of investment isn't just about creating a television show—it's about generating a media franchise that extends far beyond the television screen and into other sectors, such as merchandise, video games, and even future spin-offs.

However, the cultural investment is equally significant. The Harry Potter books and films are not merely pieces of entertainment; they are cultural landmarks. The world of Hogwarts, with its rich mythology, iconic characters, and themes of friendship, justice, and bravery, has become a touchstone for millions of people around the globe. HBO's handling of the franchise, especially in light of the controversies surrounding J.K. Rowling, will shape its cultural legacy for decades to come.

There is a fine line between honoring the original works and introducing changes that reflect contemporary cultural norms, particularly in the realms of diversity and inclusion. HBO must tread carefully, as the potential for backlash from both fans and critics is high if the series is perceived as mismanaging the franchise's moral and cultural foundations.

The show's reception will have far-reaching consequences for HBO's reputation. If the series succeeds in capturing the magic of the original while appealing to modern sensibilities, it could redefine HBO as a leader in high-quality, fan-driven television content. However, if it falters in its handling of the franchise, whether through controversial casting decisions, mishandling of beloved characters, or alienating fans with a failure to balance nostalgia and innovation, it could damage HBO's standing in the industry and erode its subscriber base.

Lessons from the Past: How Other Reboots Have Fared

The entertainment industry has seen a flood of reboots, remakes, and adaptations in recent years, with varying degrees of success. HBO's Harry Potter series is part of a larger trend of reviving beloved franchises, but it will inevitably face comparisons to other high-profile reboots. These past examples provide valuable lessons for HBO as they navigate the complexities of resurrecting an iconic property.

One notable example is the Star Wars franchise, which saw a revival with Disney's acquisition of Lucasfilm. The sequel trilogy, which began with The Force Awakens (2015), received widespread anticipation but also fierce criticism from some fans who felt the new films lacked the magic of the originals or contradicted established canon. Similarly, Star Wars has been the subject of cultural debates, especially around issues of representation and the direction of the franchise.

While some fans embraced the new direction, others rejected it, leading to a divided fandom and mixed critical reception. The key takeaway for HBO is that nostalgia alone cannot guarantee success; a reboot must strike a delicate balance between honoring the original and forging a new path that resonates with contemporary audiences.

Similarly, the Game of Thrones prequel series, House of the Dragon, also provides a relevant point of reference. After the global success of Game of Thrones, HBO was eager to capitalize on the franchise's popularity. House of the Dragon was generally well-received, but it too faced its own challenges in terms of expectations. Many fans held high hopes based on the original series, but House of the Dragon had to prove that it could stand on its own merits, even if it shared the same universe.

This series demonstrated the importance of maintaining quality storytelling, strong character development, and thoughtful engagement with the fanbase, which are lessons HBO will need to apply when adapting Harry Potter.

Other examples of reboots—such as The Lord of the Rings: The Rings of Power on Amazon Prime Video or The Witcher on Netflix—also highlight the fine line between fanservice and innovation. While Rings of Power attracted millions of viewers due to its connection to J.R.R. Tolkien's works, it also faced backlash from some fans over deviations from the source material and concerns about diversity and representation. The Witcher, based on Andrzej Sapkowski's book series, was able to navigate this challenge by staying true to the spirit of the original works while adapting them for a modern audience.

For HBO's Harry Potter series, these examples underscore the importance of making creative choices that respect the spirit of the original while introducing fresh elements that can engage modern viewers. The show will need to balance fan expectations with innovation, and avoid falling into the trap of simply repeating what has already been done.

Fans of the original books and films are incredibly vocal and protective of the material, so any misstep in casting, storytelling, or character development could result in significant backlash. At the same time, however, the success of these reboots demonstrates that there is still immense value in the Harry Potter franchise, if the series can deliver a well-crafted, thoughtful adaptation that resonates with a diverse, contemporary audience.

Ultimately, HBO's Harry Potter series will stand as one of the most ambitious and high-stakes reboots in recent memory, with the potential to reshape the future of streaming and franchise television. By learning from past successes and failures, HBO has the opportunity to create a legacy-defining television series that both honors the past and embraces the future.

CHAPTER TEN

A Look Ahead to 2027 and Beyond

As the Harry Potter television series heads into its development phase with a targeted release window of 2027, early projections for its success are a mix of optimism and caution. The potential for global viewership is immense, given the widespread popularity of the Harry Potter franchise, which continues to engage millions through books, films, video games, and theme parks.

The series' success seems all but guaranteed in terms of initial viewership, but maintaining that momentum over seven seasons will be the true test of HBO's ability to deliver an engaging and faithful adaptation.

HBO's ambitious plan to structure the series as a seven-season epic, each aligned with one of the seven books, is a bold move. In an age where binge-watching dominates viewing habits, Harry Potter must balance the expectations of both new viewers who might be unfamiliar with the original material and die-hard fans who are invested in every detail of the books.

Early projections from industry analysts suggest that the series could be a cornerstone for HBO's future in the streaming wars, bringing in a new wave of subscribers and drawing in viewers globally. With each season potentially involving a staggering production budget and a carefully crafted global marketing strategy, the show's financial impact is expected to be significant.

However, as much as the show is positioned for success, challenges loom. A reboot of this scale will inevitably face heightened scrutiny, both from longtime fans and critics alike. The adaptation of beloved characters, the portrayal of key moments, and the show's treatment of sensitive issues like diversity, inclusion, and the handling of J.K. Rowling's legacy will all factor into its reception.

The success of the show will not only depend on viewer ratings but also on cultural acceptance and its ability to engage with the current societal landscape in a way that feels both authentic and forward-thinking.

Moreover, in terms of critical success, early projections indicate that the series must not only measure up to the Harry Potter films but also match or exceed the quality of other high-budget series in the fantasy genre, like Game of Thrones and The Witcher. For HBO, ensuring the series' reputation extends beyond just financial profits and into critical acclaim will be pivotal in securing its place in television history.

The Evolution of the Harry Potter Legacy: A New Chapter Begins

The release of the Harry Potter series in 2027 marks not just the beginning of a new chapter in the franchise but also the evolution of the legacy that J.K. Rowling created more than two decades ago. The books and films have already made an indelible mark on popular culture, and the upcoming television series offers a chance to expand that impact in new and exciting ways. The franchise's continued relevance in a rapidly changing media landscape speaks to the lasting power of its central themes of friendship, courage, and the battle between good and evil.

What makes this adaptation particularly exciting is the opportunity to explore the Harry Potter universe in greater depth. While the films were beloved, they necessarily condensed much of the source material, leaving some fans yearning for a more comprehensive exploration of the Wizarding World.

The TV series, with its longer runtime and the ability to break down each book into multiple episodes, promises to give fans a more expansive and detailed look at key events, character arcs, and the intricate magical systems that have become so beloved. This deeper dive into the world of Hogwarts also opens the door for exploring subplots and minor characters that were previously sidelined, offering fans a new perspective on the story.

Beyond the immediate world of Hogwarts, the series will also have the opportunity to explore the broader Wizarding World in a way that the films didn't. With the original films largely focused on Harry, Ron, and Hermione's journey, the show has a chance to expand on the history of magical communities, the wider political landscape of the wizarding world, and other magical beings and creatures.

Such expansive storytelling will undoubtedly evolve the legacy of the franchise, making it not only a rehash of the beloved series but also an opportunity to expand the Harry Potter universe in ways that are both nostalgic and novel.

Culturally, the series will influence not just future adaptations of literary works but also the wider world of fantasy media. Harry Potter has long been recognized for its imaginative storytelling, its ability to blend magical escapism with universal moral lessons, and its portrayal of complex characters. As the series enters this new era, it will undoubtedly continue to shape how magical worlds are perceived in contemporary media, potentially setting the bar for future fantasy adaptations.

Speculation and Hopes: What Fans Want from Seven Seasons

Fans of the Harry Potter series have high expectations for the upcoming television adaptation, and with good reason. The books have captured the imaginations of millions around the world, and the films created an iconic portrayal of J.K. Rowling's world. The pressure on HBO is immense to not only deliver a faithful adaptation but also to exceed the expectations of a fanbase that is protective of the source material.

There are several aspects that fans are most excited about, and, conversely, the elements they are nervous about. First and foremost, the fidelity to the original source material is critical. Fans expect the show to stay true to the books, especially in the portrayal of beloved characters, key events, and overarching themes.

The depth of the characters, from the heroic trio of Harry, Ron, and Hermione to the complex antagonists like Voldemort and Draco Malfoy, is essential to the success of the series. Fans are hoping to see these characters developed more fully than in the films, especially with the ability to dedicate more time to each character's backstory, growth, and relationships.

Another expectation from fans is the handling of major story arcs and themes, particularly those that explore love, sacrifice, and the nuances of good versus evil. The emotional depth of Harry Potter is one of its strongest aspects, and fans hope the series will capture this emotional resonance.

Moments like the battle at Hogwarts, the deaths of key characters, and Harry's journey of self-discovery all demand a careful balance of respect for the original narrative while ensuring that the portrayal is fresh and emotionally impactful for a new generation of viewers.

In addition, fans are also excited about the possibility of new characters and deeper explorations of the Wizarding World that the series can offer. The chance to dive into the rich history of magic, the mysterious past of Hogwarts, and the untold stories of secondary characters such as Neville Longbottom, Luna Lovegood, and the Weasley family has generated much anticipation. These characters have loyal fan followings, and expanding their stories will be a rewarding challenge for the creative team.

However, some fans are wary about certain aspects of the new series, particularly when it comes to issues like casting, diversity, and the potential for changes to the storyline that may feel inconsistent with the books.

Many fans are protective of how the franchise portrays its core characters, and any major deviations or reinterpretations could lead to backlash. J.K. Rowling's involvement, particularly given the controversies surrounding her comments on transgender issues, also raises concerns for many fans. Some fear that her presence in the production could negatively impact the tone and messages of the show, especially when it comes to diversity and representation.

The hope is that HBO's Harry Potter series will balance these concerns and create something that both honors the legacy of the original books and films while offering a new, exciting interpretation for a modern audience. Fans want a show that respects the magic and charm of the original works while pushing the boundaries of what is possible in a television adaptation of such a beloved and complex world.

Ultimately, the success of the Harry Potter series will come down to the ability of HBO to meet these high expectations. The show has the potential to redefine the Harry Potter legacy for a new era, but only if it can live up to the immense pressure placed on its shoulders. For fans, it's a journey they're eager to take, with hopes that the magic that enchanted them years ago will once again capture their hearts in a fresh and exciting way.

CONCLUSION

The Power of Stories: Why the New Harry Potter Series Matters

The upcoming Harry Potter television series is more than just an adaptation of a beloved book series; it represents the enduring power of stories to shape our culture and our lives.

The Harry Potter saga has been a defining narrative of the 21st century, captivating generations of readers and moviegoers with its magical world, unforgettable characters, and universal themes of love, friendship, courage, and the battle against darkness. As the series makes its transition from film to television, its continued significance is undeniable.

What makes this new series particularly impactful is not just the nostalgia it will evoke in long-time fans but the new opportunities it presents to explore deeper, more nuanced aspects of the Wizarding World. In an era when media consumption is rapidly evolving, the chance to revisit and expand upon Harry Potter through a long-form format allows for a richer exploration of characters, subplots, and themes that could not fully be explored in the films.

The series, while maintaining its connection to the magical legacy that made it iconic, will also offer fresh perspectives and engage new generations in ways the original books and films may not have been able to.

At its core, the Harry Potter series is about more than just magic; it's about the power of storytelling itself. It's about how stories can shape our worldview, provide solace in difficult times, and inspire us to become better versions of ourselves.

The new series has the potential to rekindle the magic that so many fans experienced the first time they encountered the books and films and to share that magic with a whole new audience. This power is why the series, regardless of its controversies or challenges, will continue to matter—both in the world of entertainment and in the lives of those who continue to find meaning in its themes.

Bridging the Gap: Fandom, Inclusion, and the Magic of Adaptation

As the Harry Potter series moves into its next chapter, it faces both the weight of its legacy and the need to adapt to an evolving cultural landscape. The adaptation of such a cherished story is never without its challenges, but the opportunity to bridge the gap between long-time fans and new generations is significant. The importance of this new series lies not only in how it honors the original works but also in how it engages with modern issues surrounding fandom, inclusion, and representation.

One of the central concerns for many fans of the Harry Potter universe is how the series will address the cultural context of the present day, especially given the controversies surrounding J.K. Rowling's views on gender and transgender rights. These issues have sparked heated debates within the fandom, dividing opinions on whether or not it is possible to separate the art from the artist.

For some, the presence of Rowling's personal views in the public sphere is a difficult obstacle to overcome, while for others, her role as creator cannot be disregarded. The new series must navigate this delicate balance, taking care to present a show that remains faithful to the inclusive, compassionate messages of the books while respecting the sensitivities of a diverse modern audience.

Inclusivity in casting, storytelling, and representation will be critical in determining the series' cultural relevance. HBO's promise of inclusive, diverse casting is a step in the right direction, but it must be more than a token gesture. True inclusivity means ensuring that all aspects of the show—from character development to plotlines—reflect the values of the society in which it is being made. I

n a world where diversity is an increasingly important conversation in media, the Harry Potter series can either serve as a model for progress or fall short if it fails to address these concerns thoughtfully.

Adaptation, in its purest form, is about transformation—about taking something familiar and remaking it into something that speaks to the current moment. The Harry Potter series stands at the crossroads of nostalgia and progress, and how it navigates that intersection will determine its place in history.

By addressing the complexities of modern fandom, acknowledging the need for inclusive representation, and balancing the rich tradition of the books with the demands of contemporary audiences, the series has the opportunity to further elevate the Harry Potter legacy in a way that feels both timeless and of the moment.

The magic of adaptation lies in its ability to take the core of a beloved story and breathe new life into it, making it relevant to the world as it exists today. The new Harry Potter series has the potential to do just that: to remain true to the heart of what made the books so beloved while offering a new, nuanced, and inclusive take on the Wizarding World.

This delicate dance between honoring the past and embracing the future will be what ultimately defines the series. The magic that fans have loved for over two decades is still very much alive—it's just waiting to be rediscovered and reimagined for a new generation. Through careful crafting, thoughtful adaptation, and respect for the diverse audience it now serves, the series can once again cast its spell on the world.

In this way, the new Harry Potter series is not just a continuation of a story—it's a vital part of the ongoing conversation about culture, media, and the role of storytelling in shaping society. And, in the end, that is the real magic.

The Complete Inside Story of HBO's Most Anticipated Show

THANKS FOR READING!!!